TRAINS

Coloring Book

For Adults

SPARKS IDEA
CREATIVE GENERATION

This Book Belongs To:

Color tester

Cover and Images by:
Vecteezy.com Freepik.com

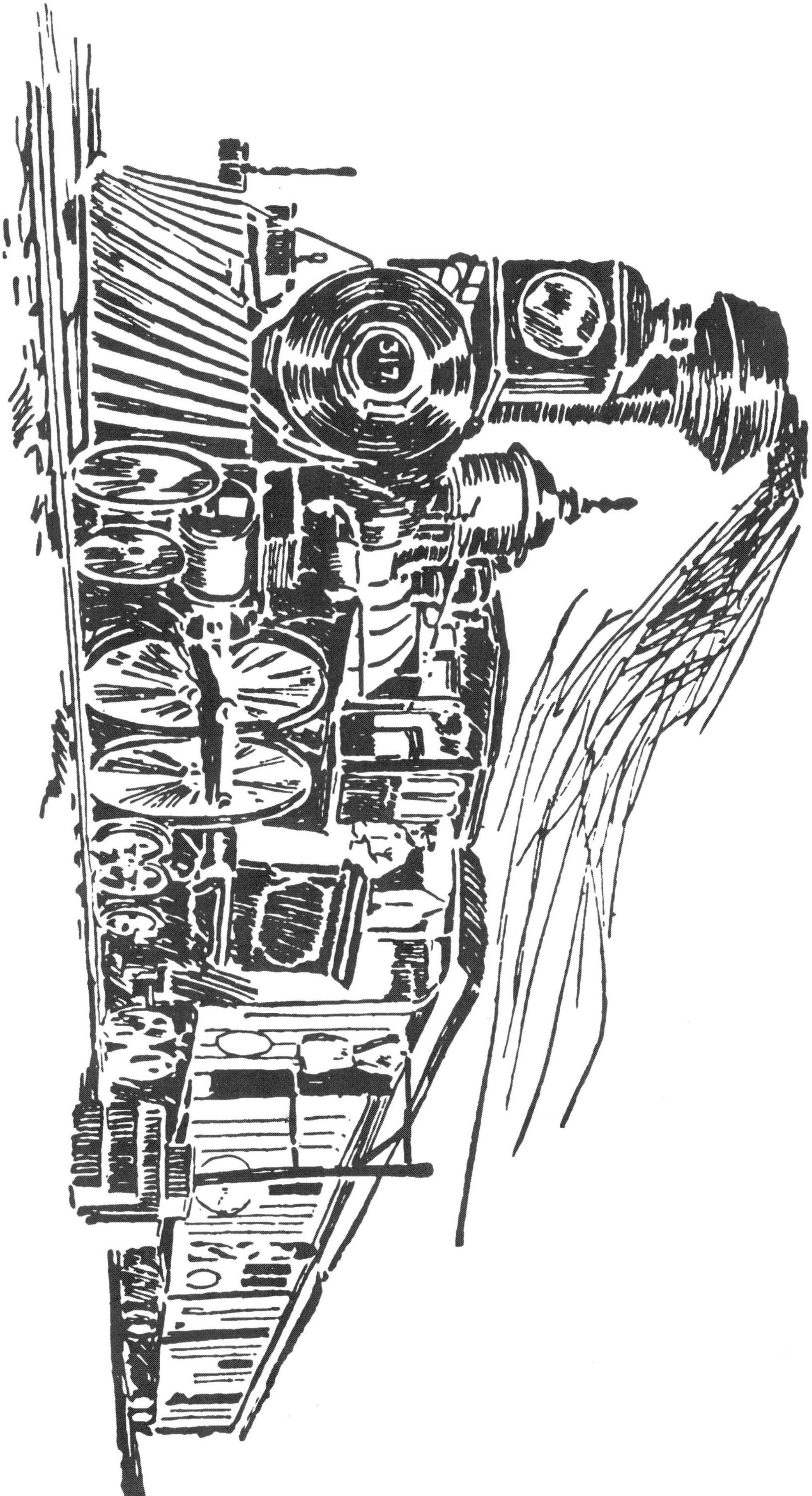
317

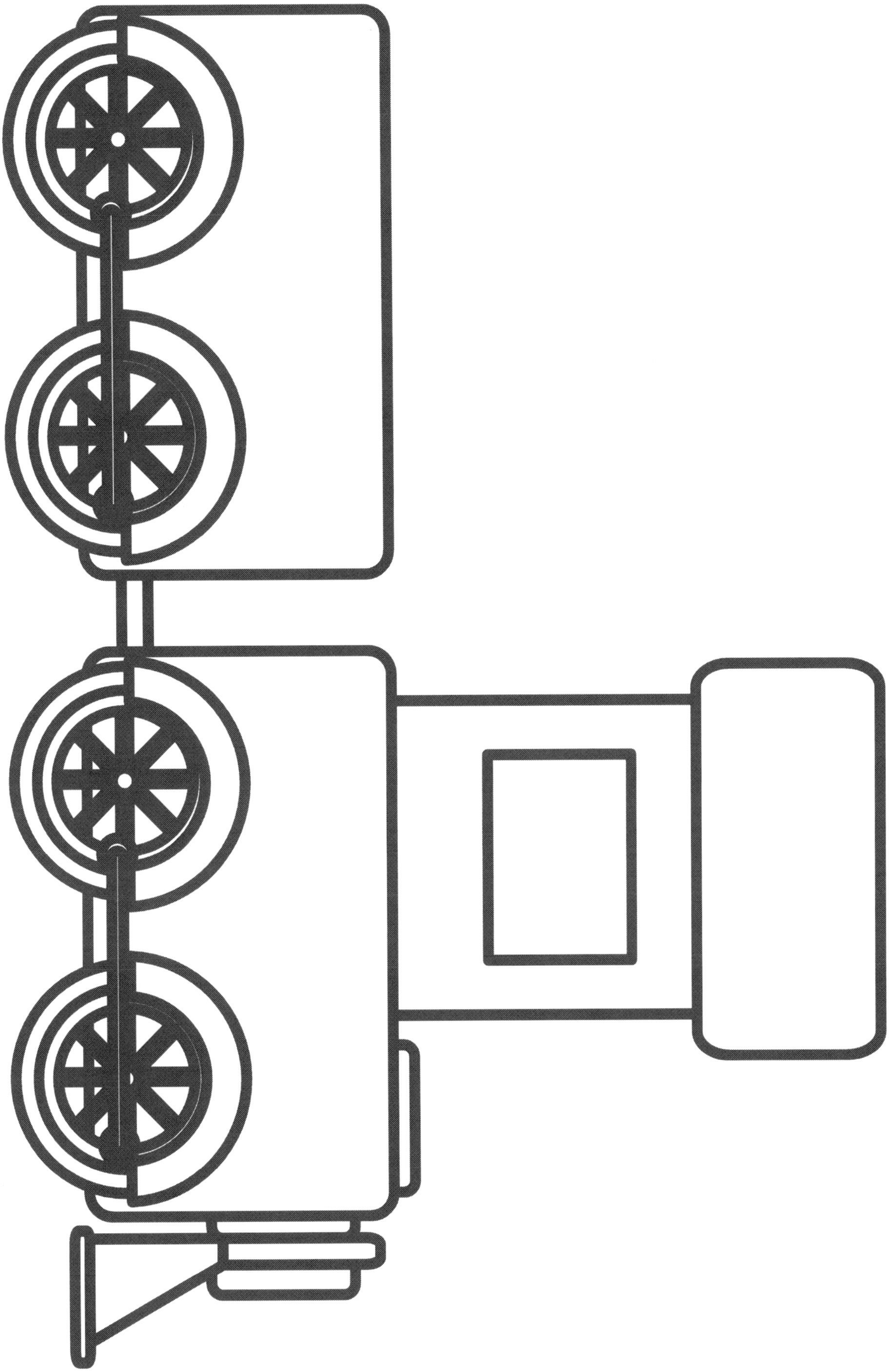

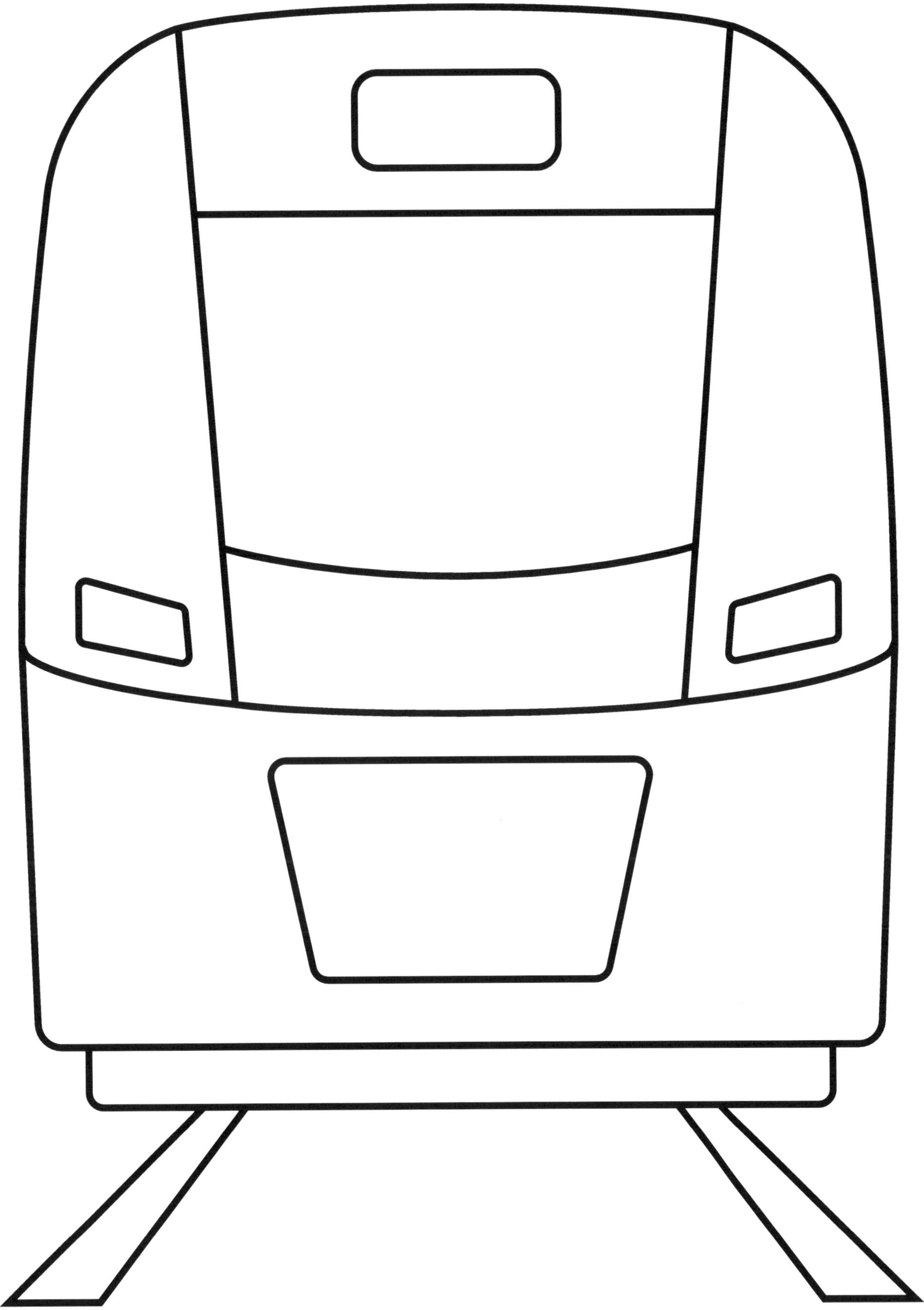

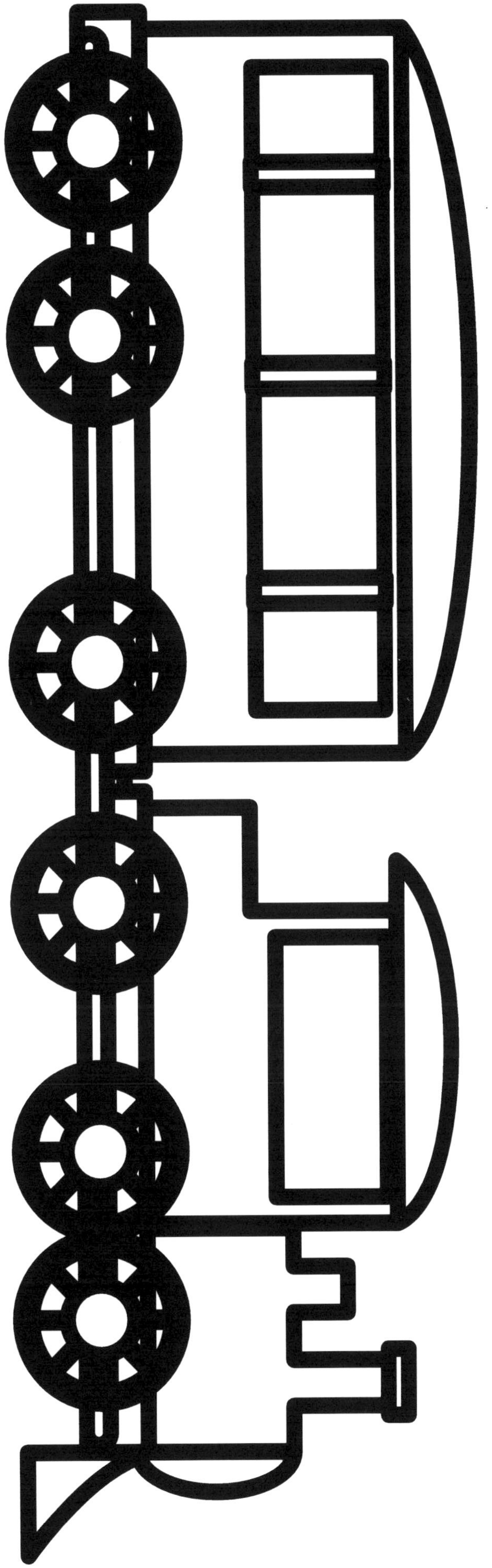

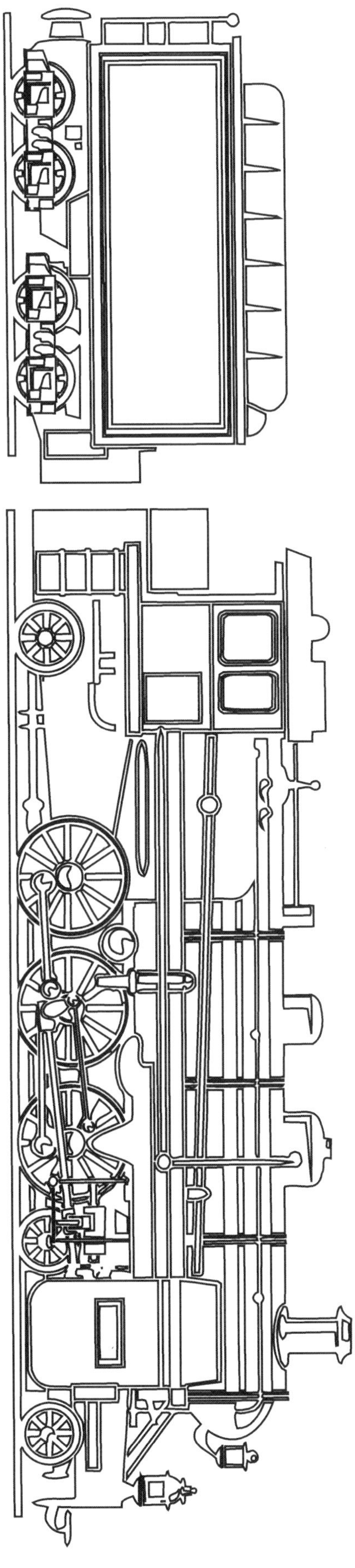

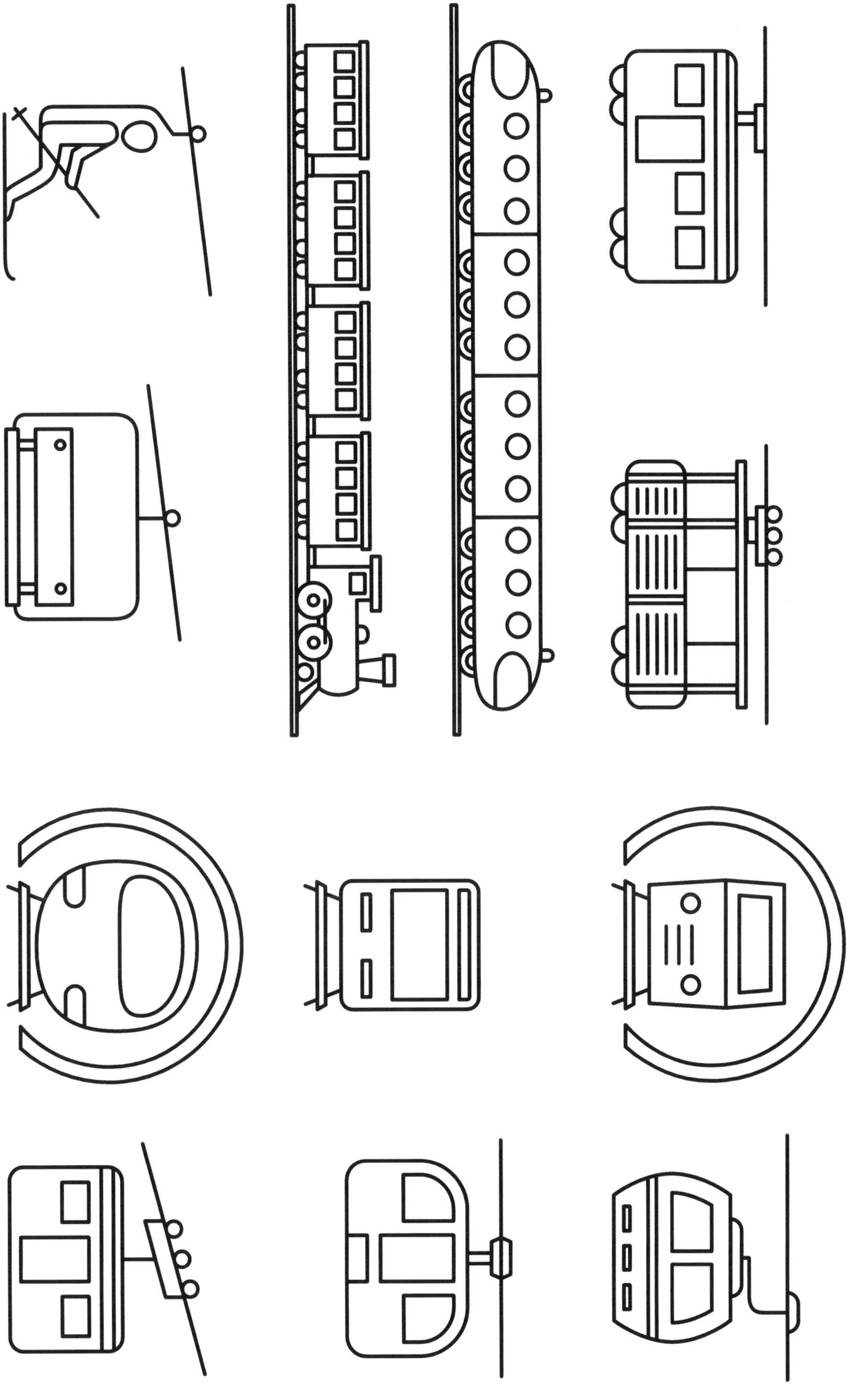

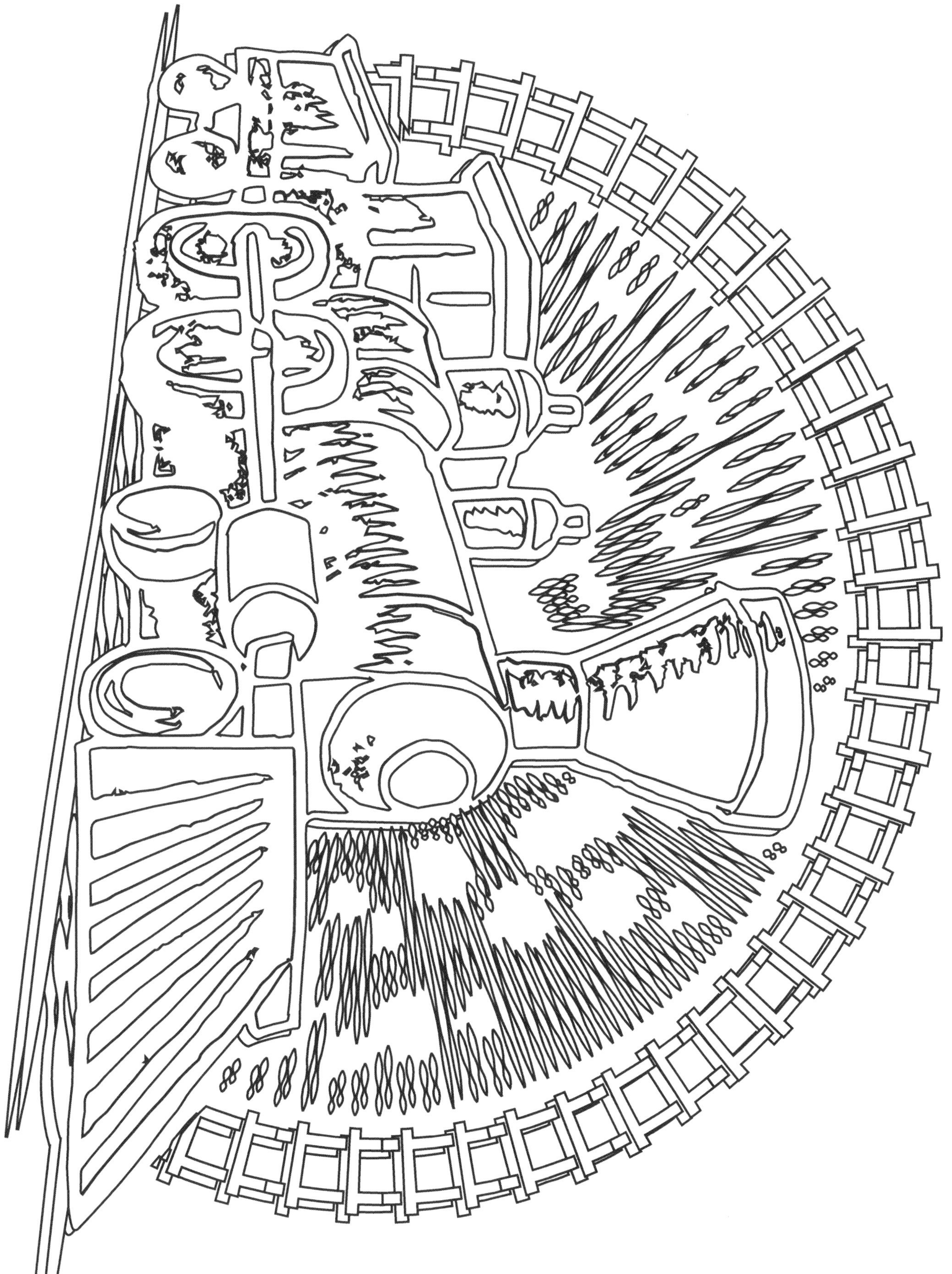

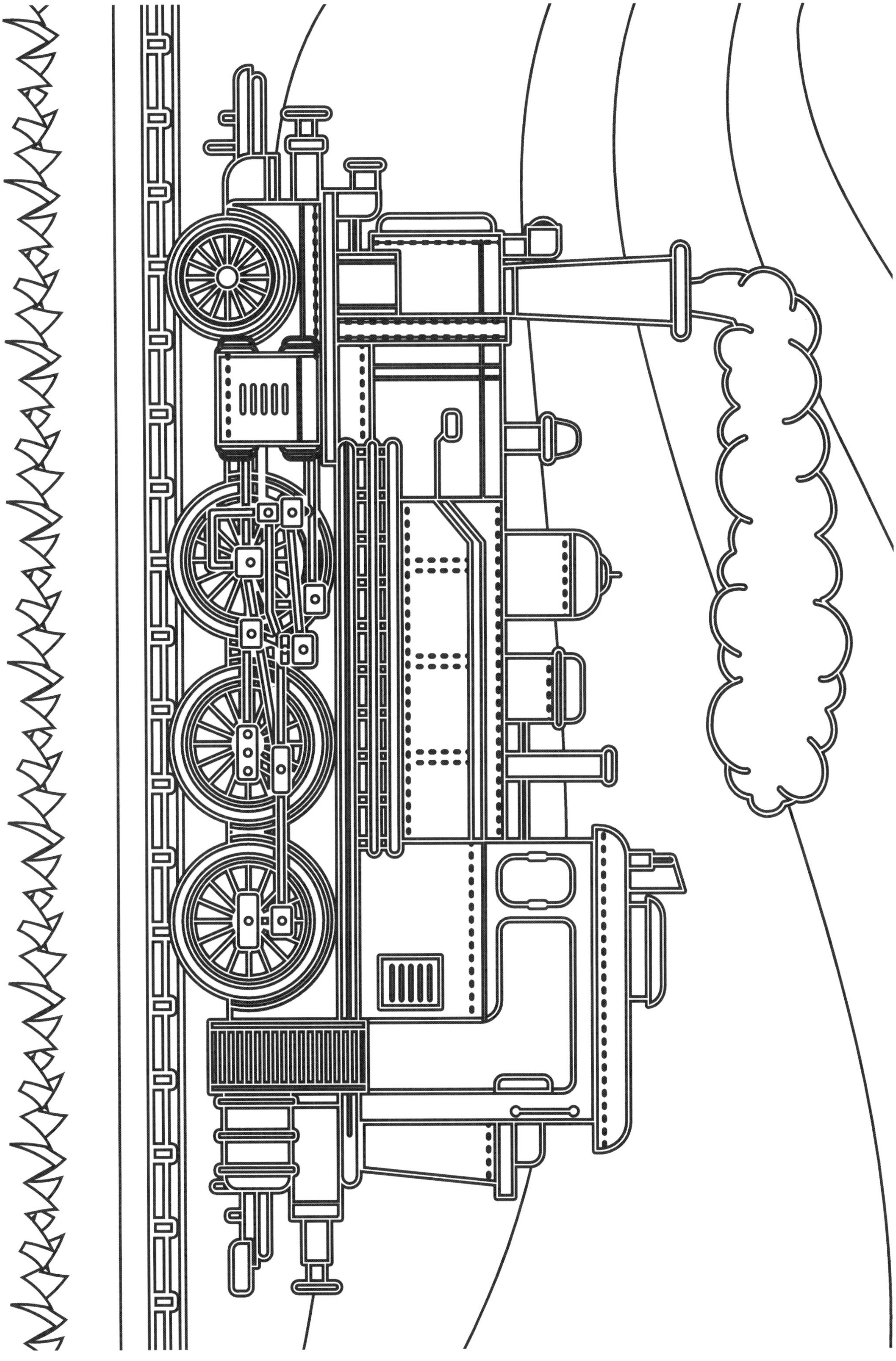

RED CABOOSE
C2344
02
02

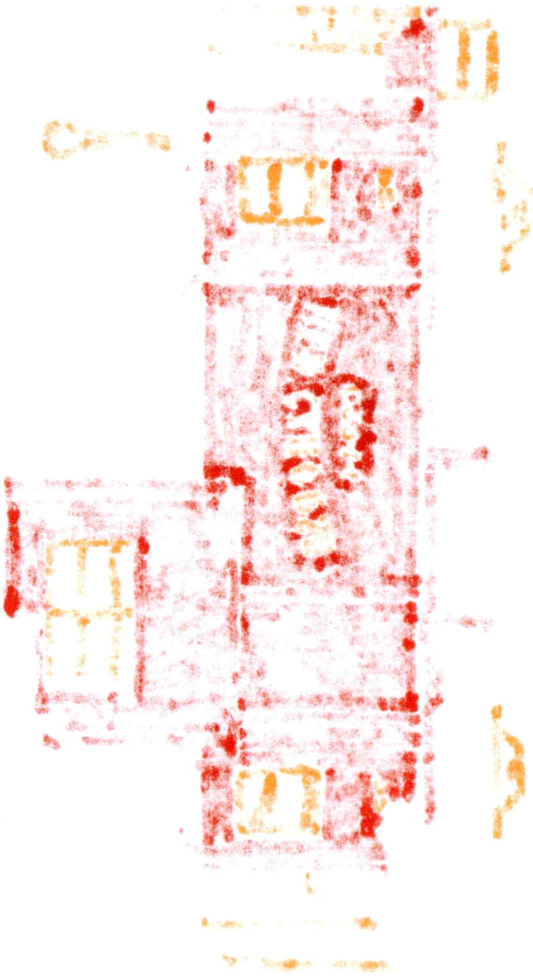

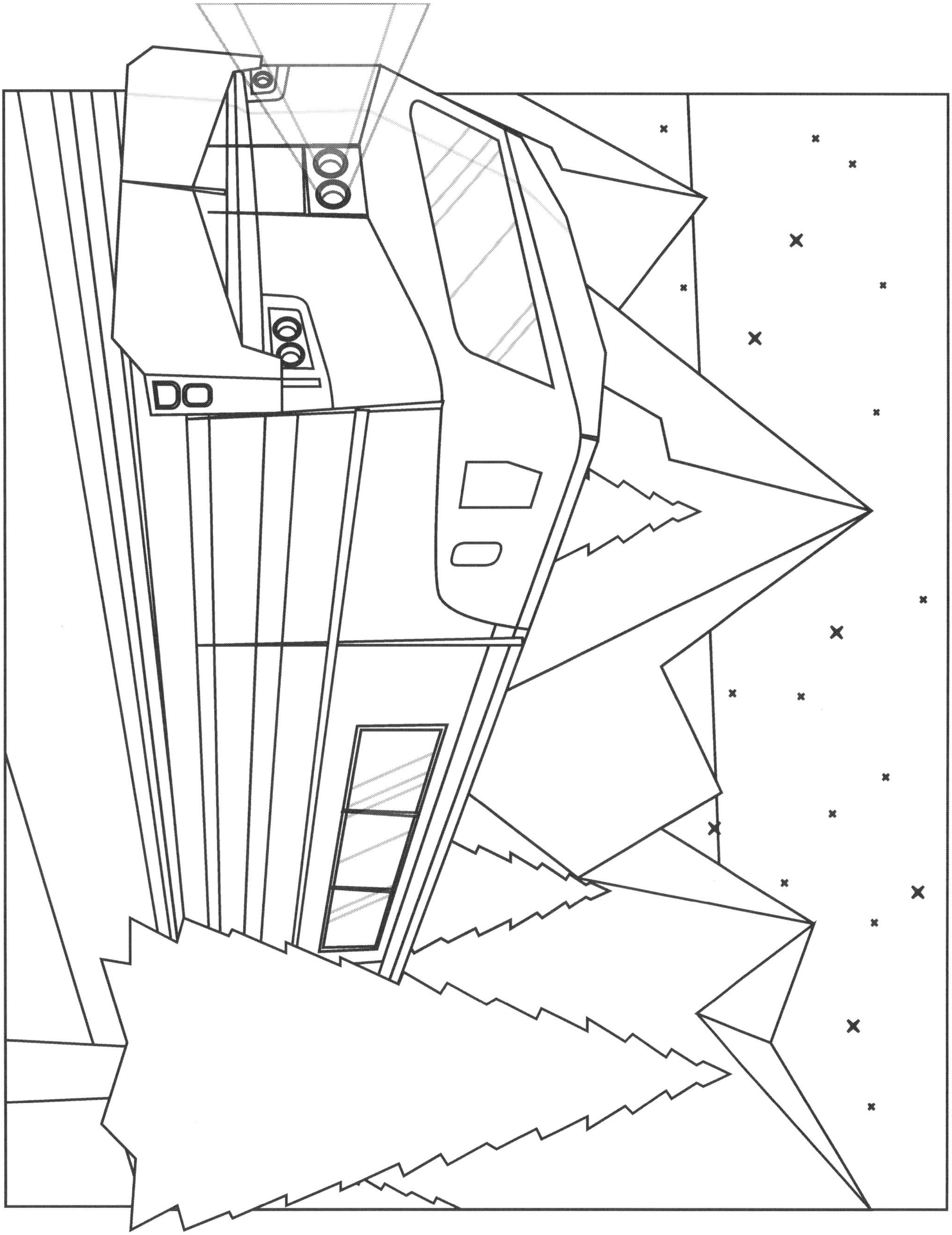
DO

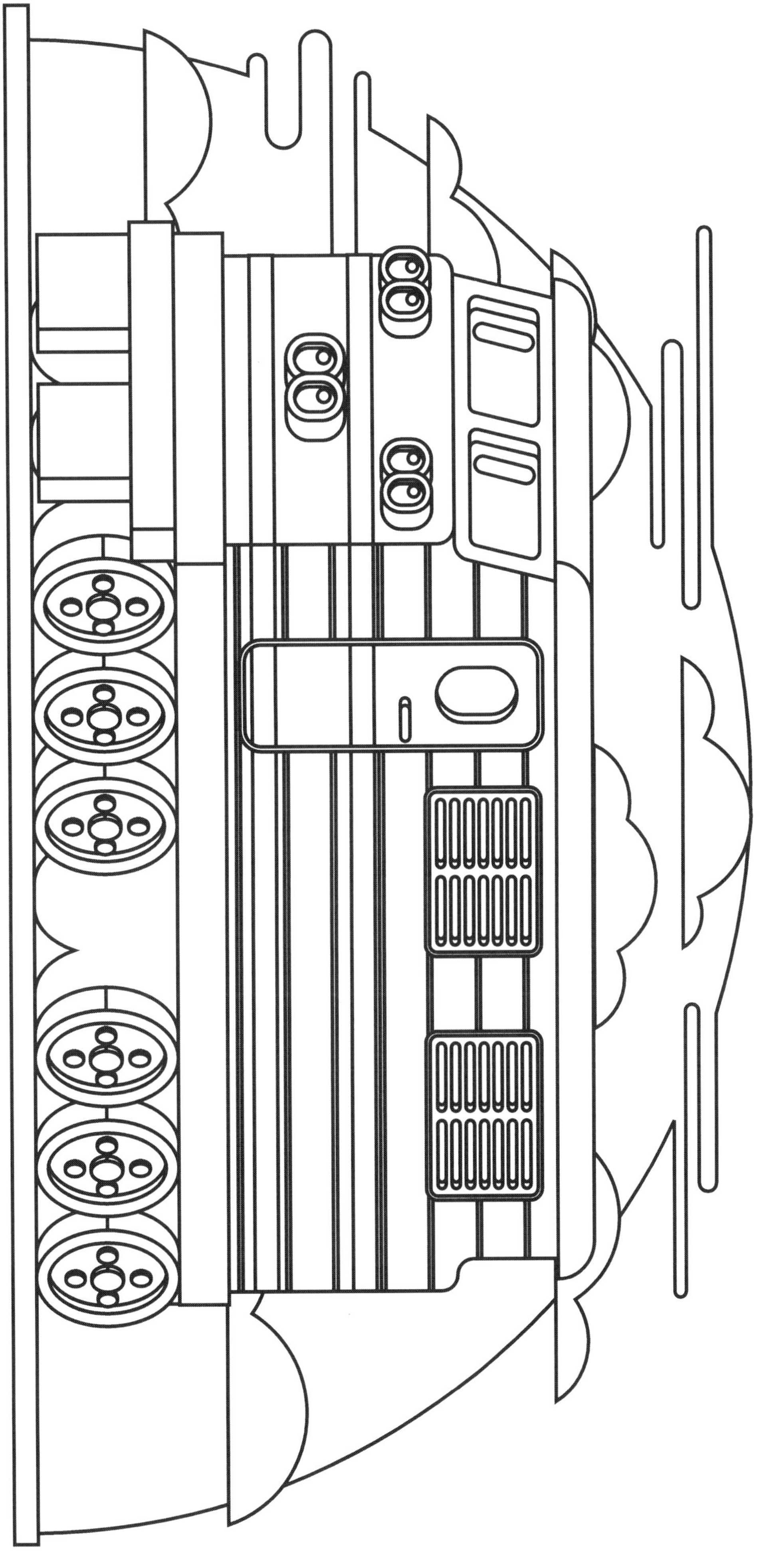

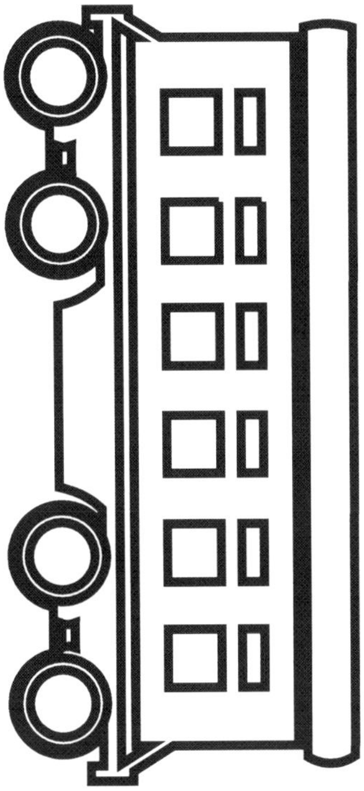
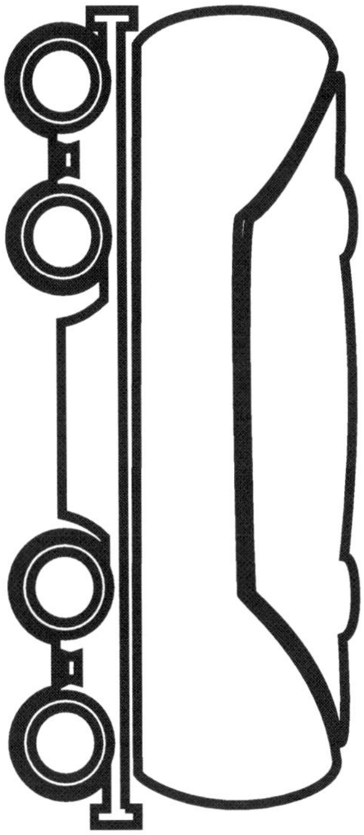
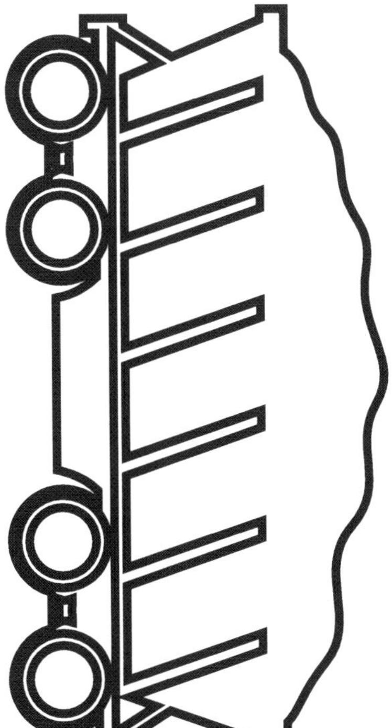
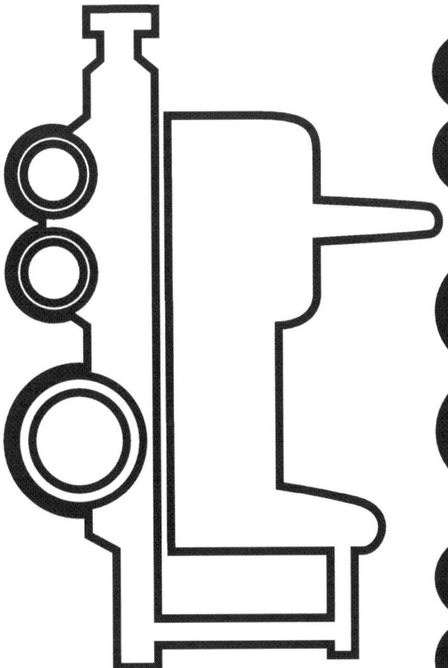
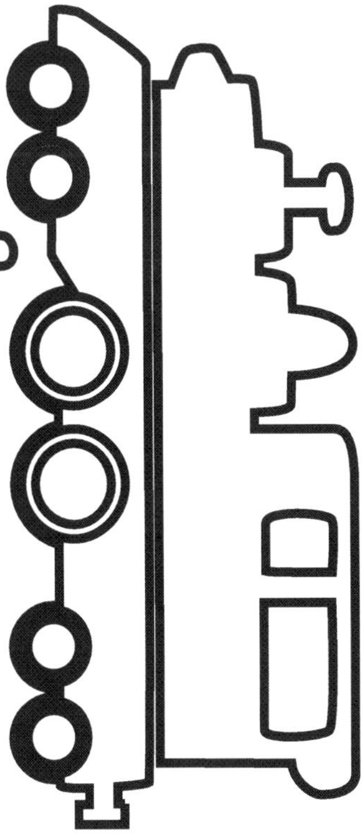

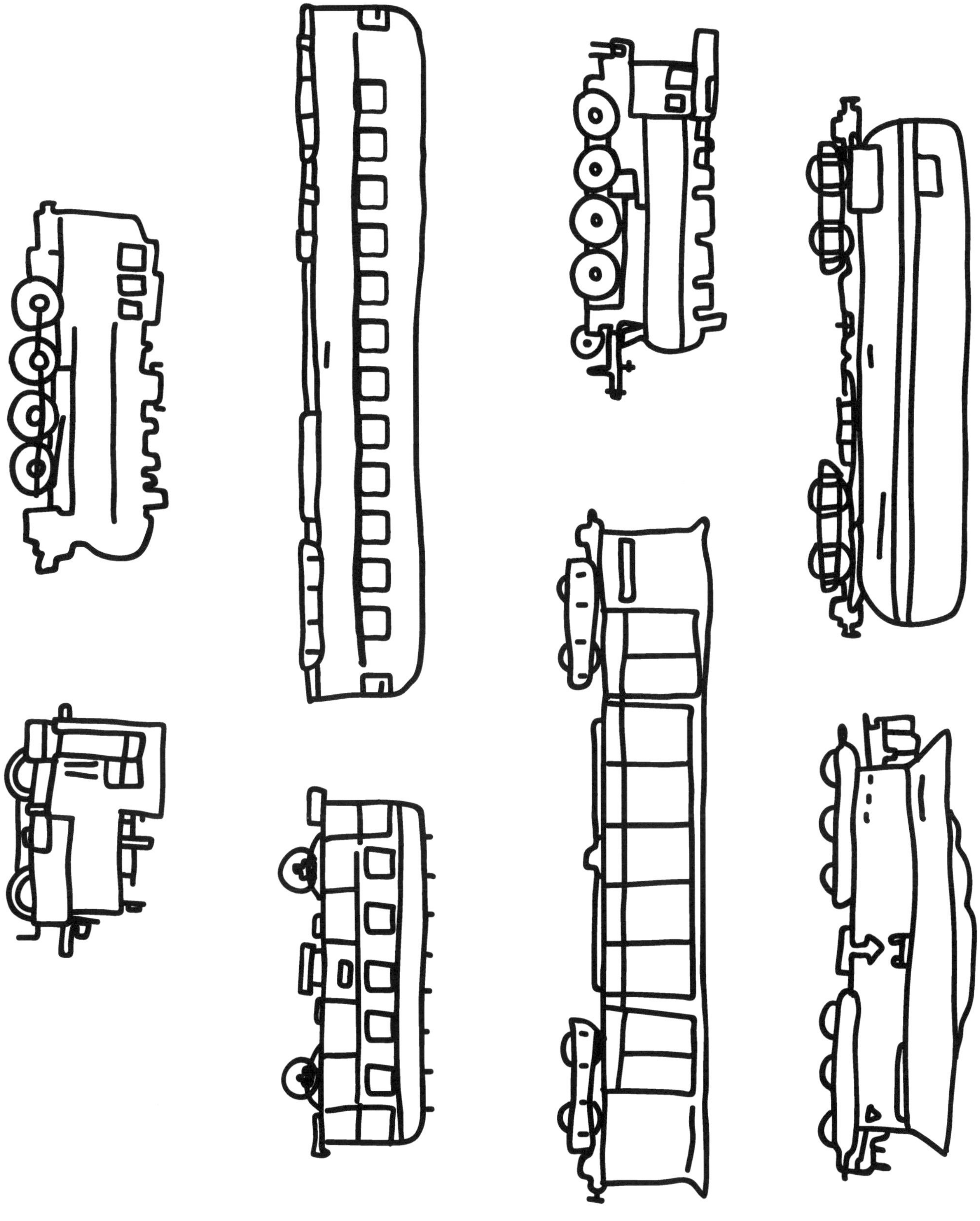

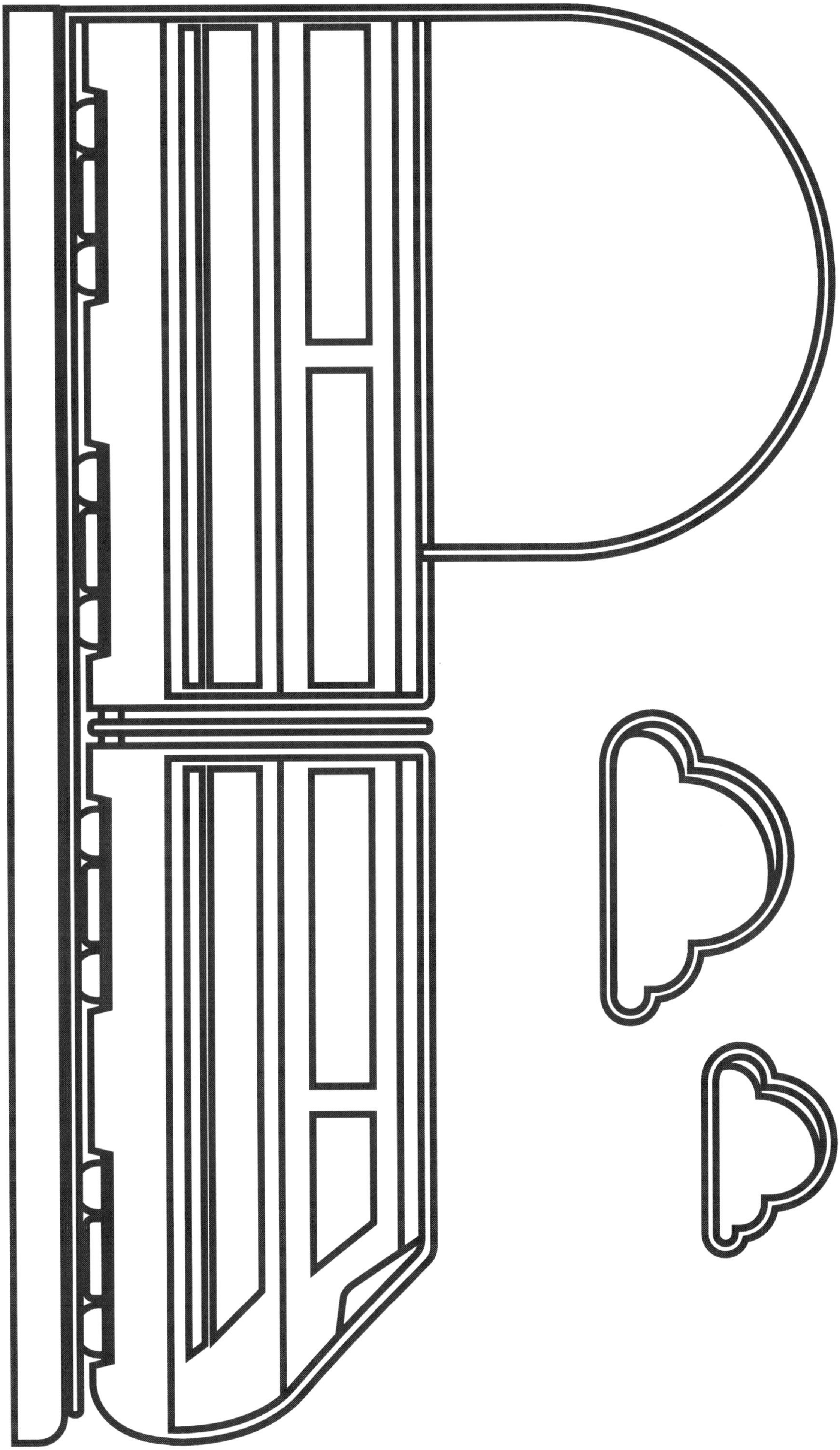

Dutout Op
hot.

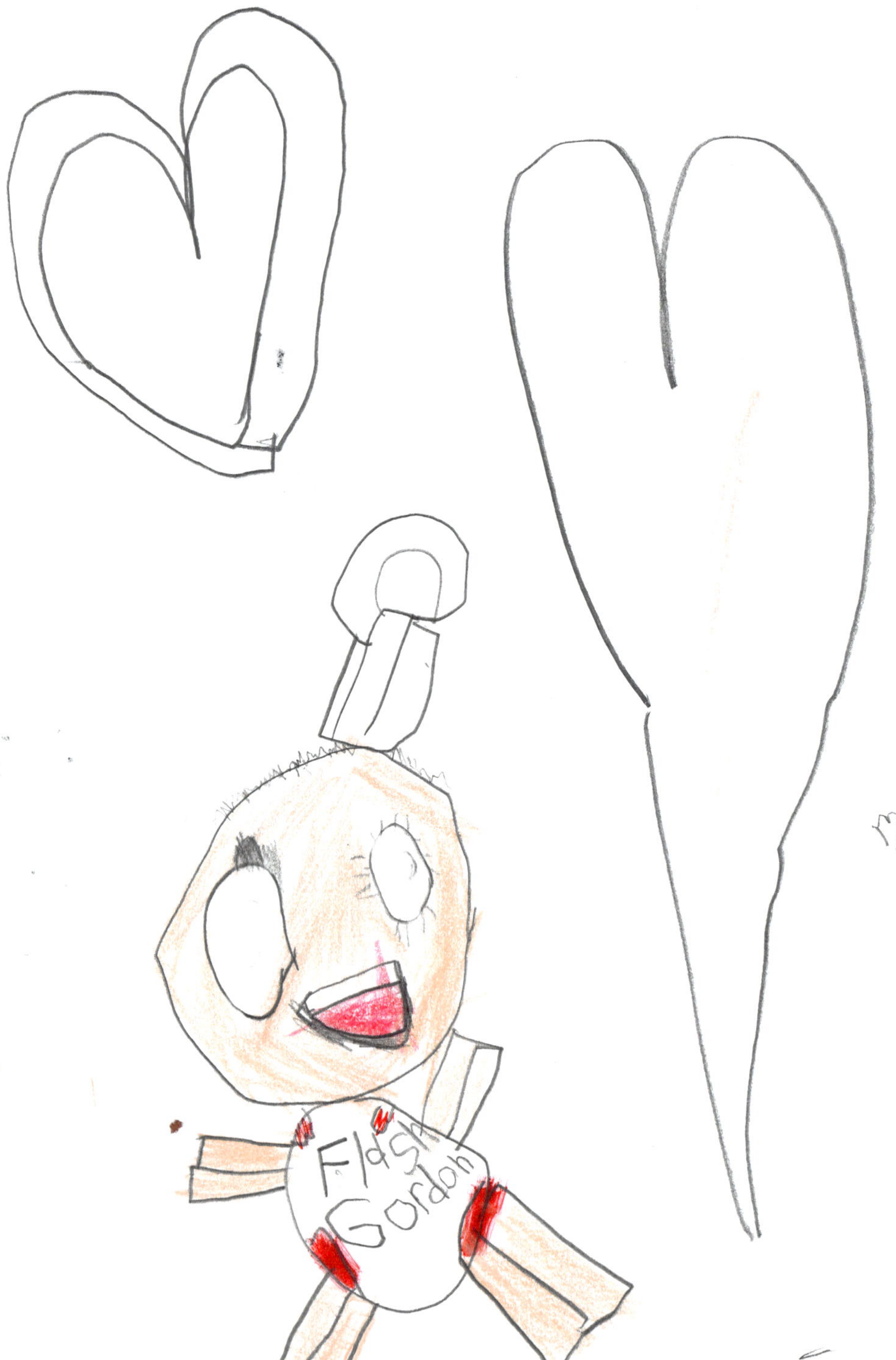
Flash Gordon

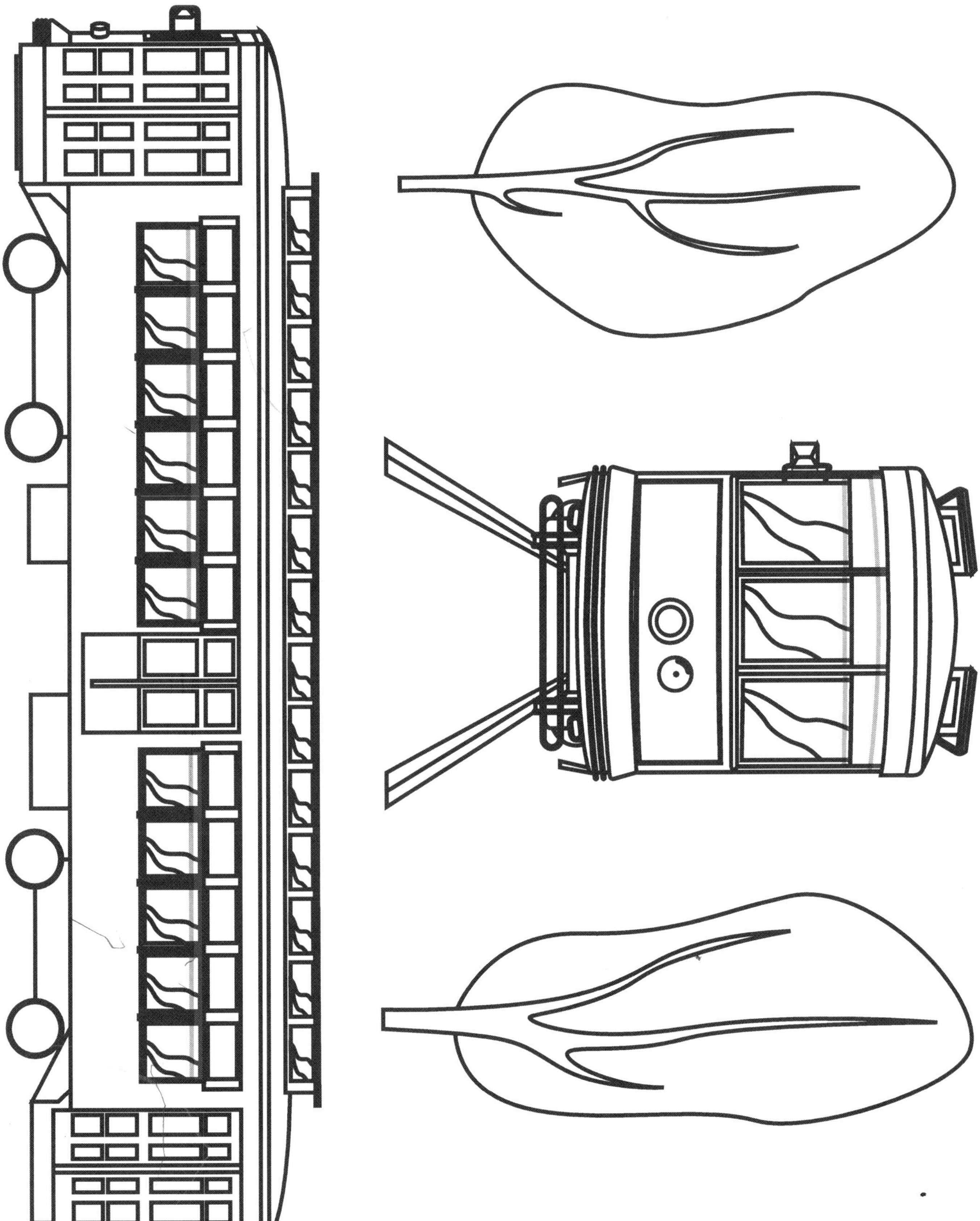

CABOOSE

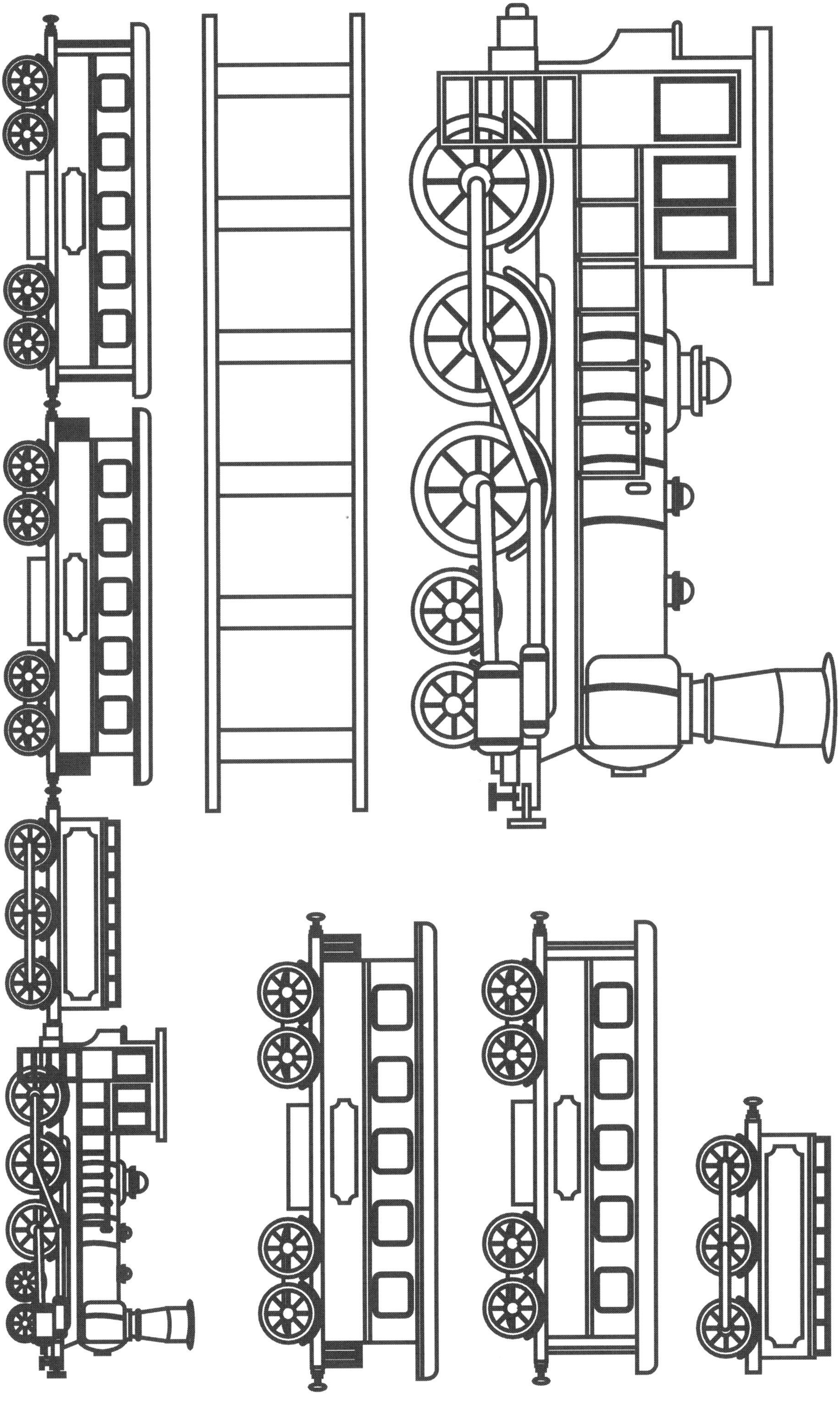

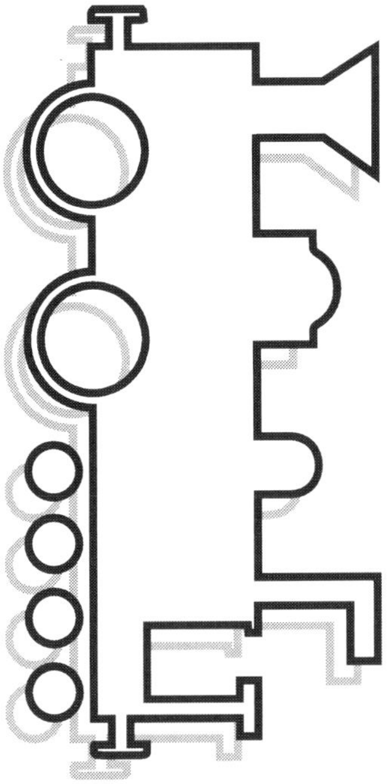

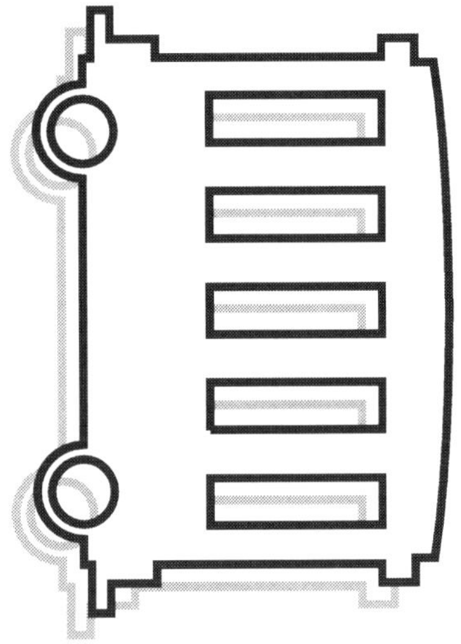

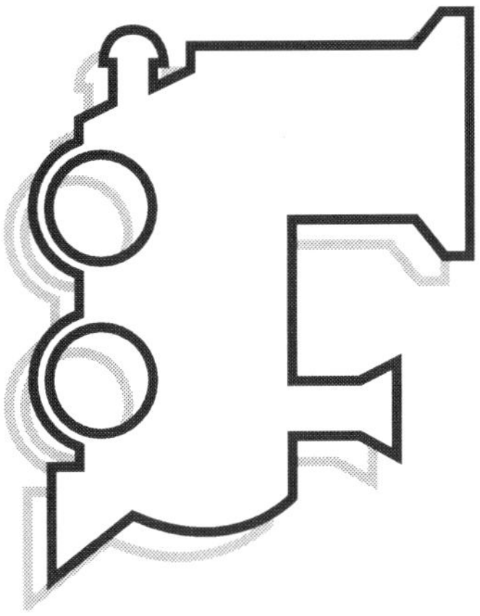

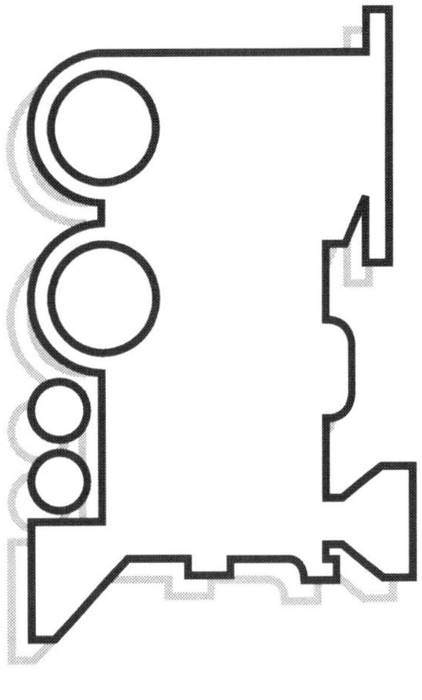

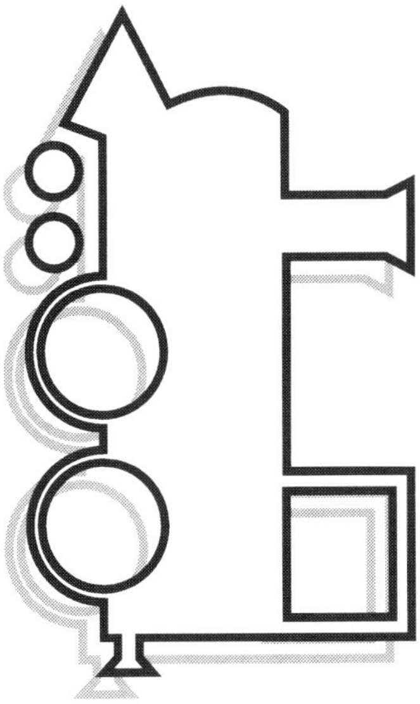

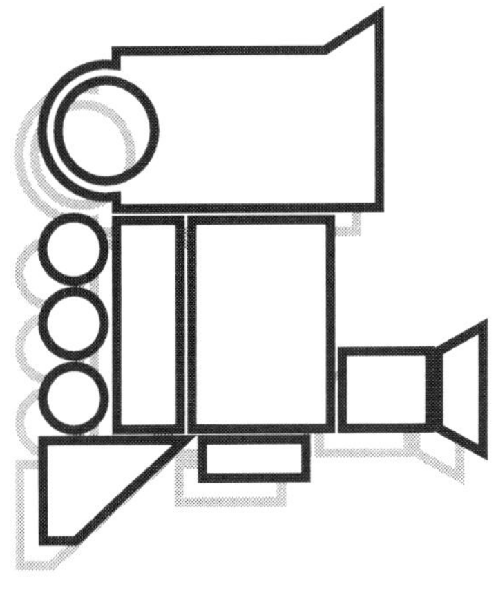

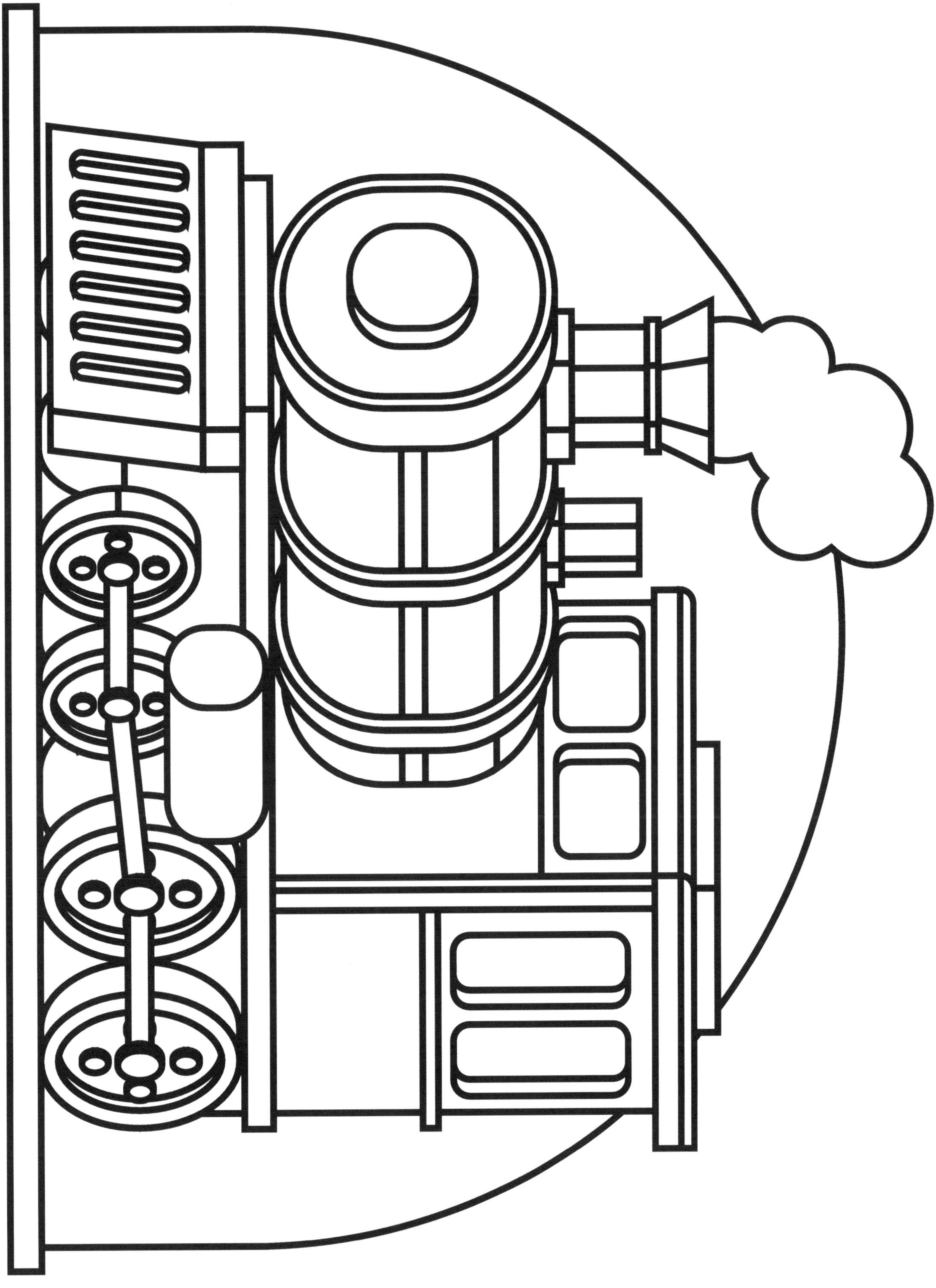

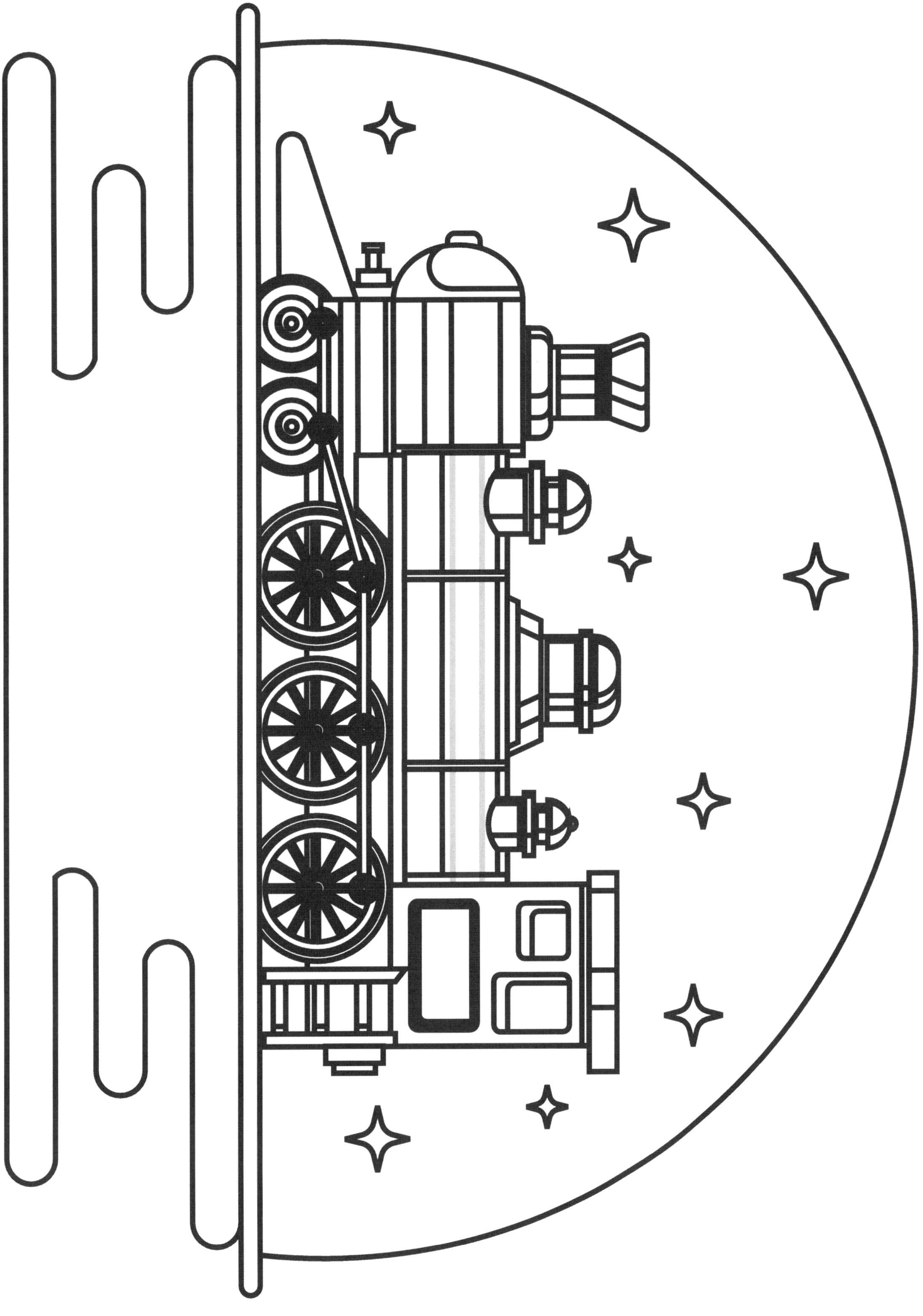

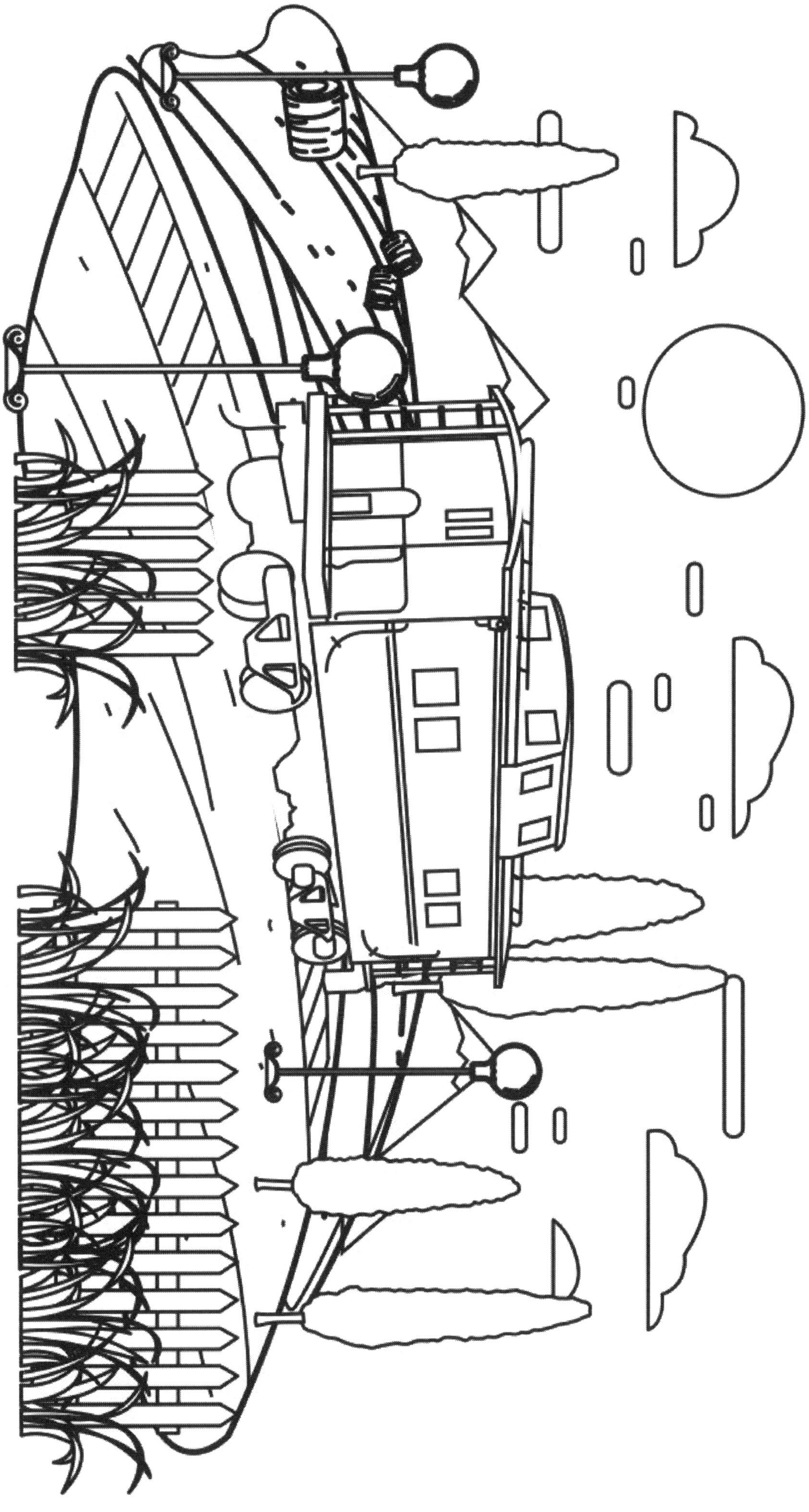

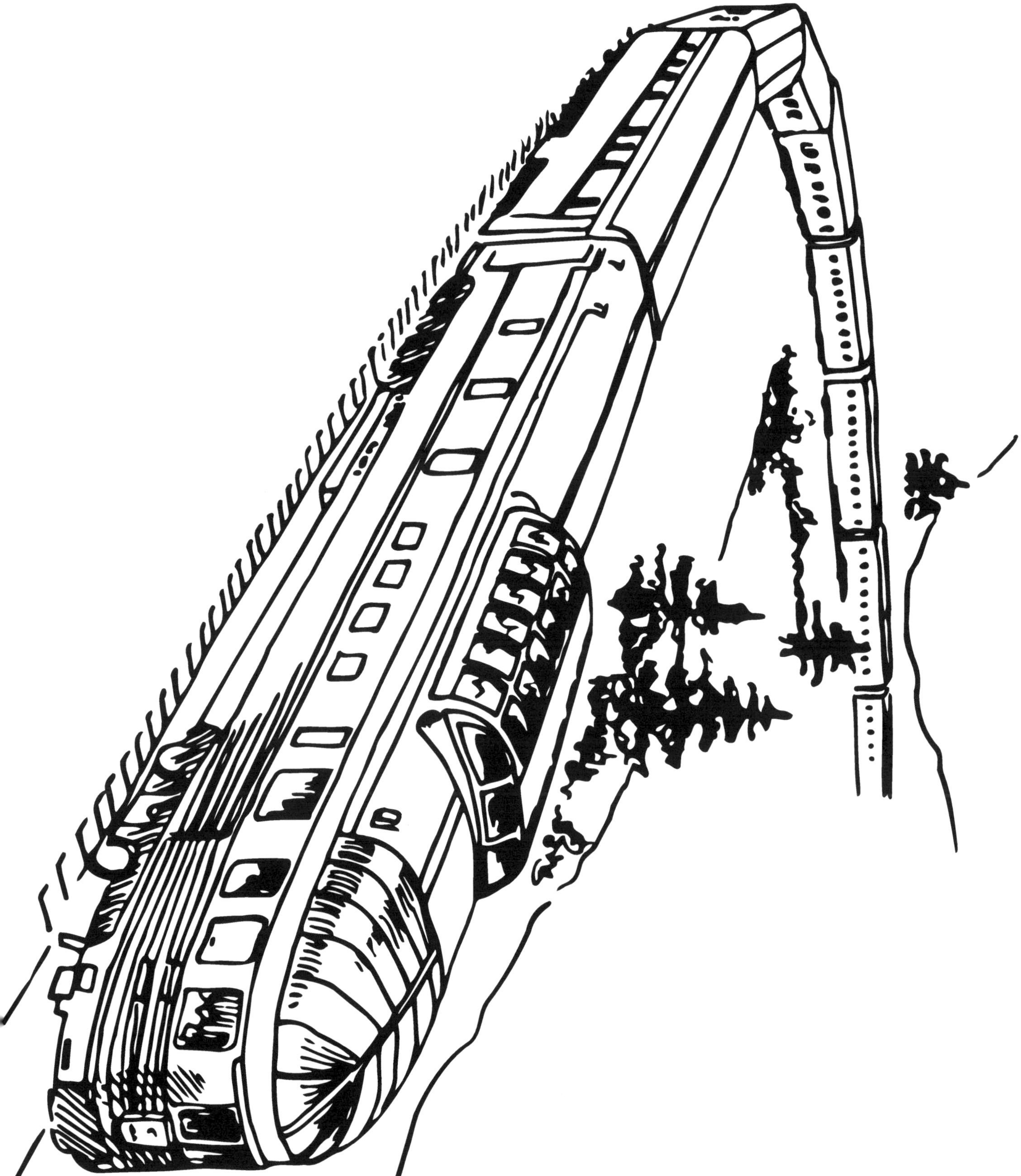

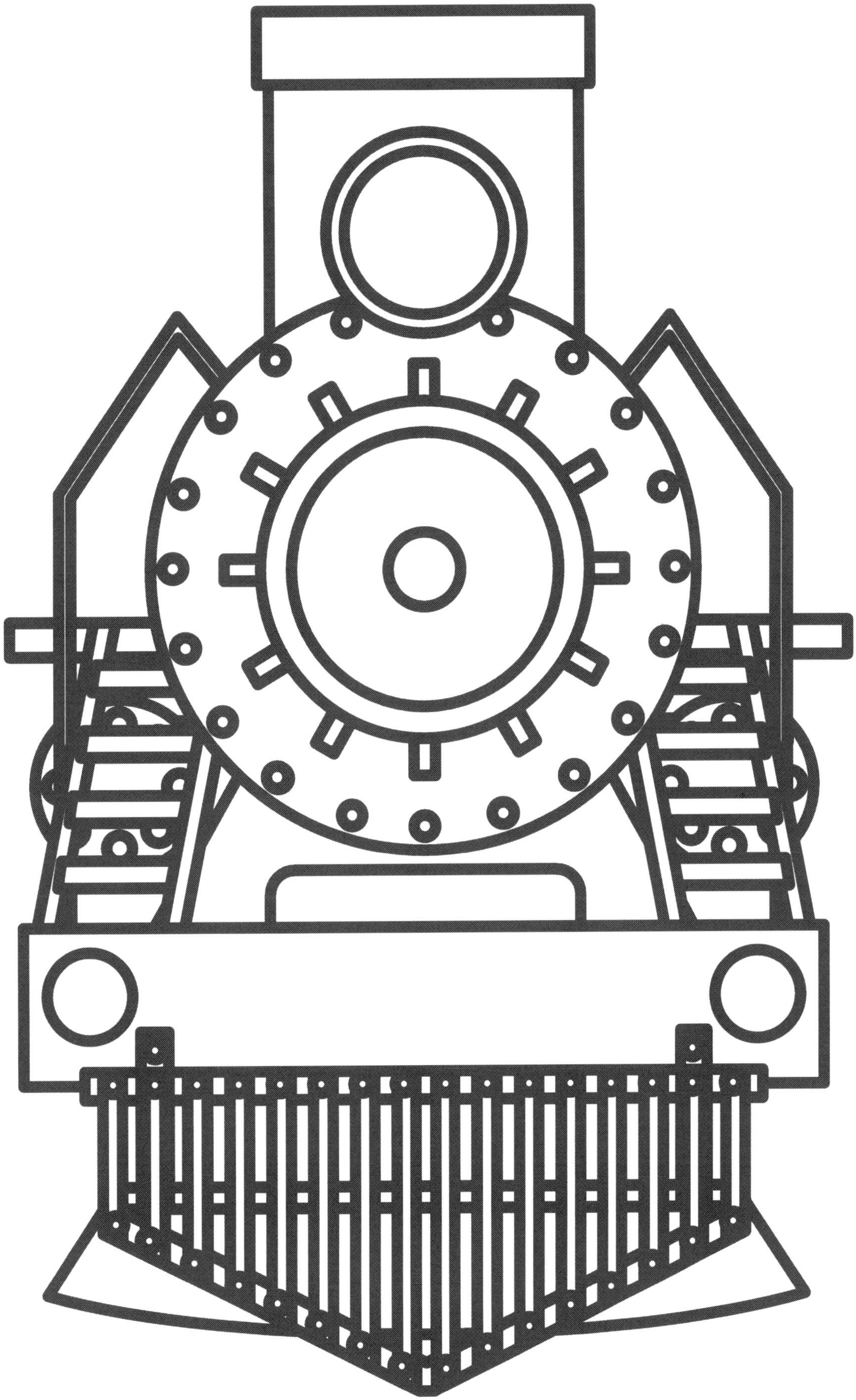

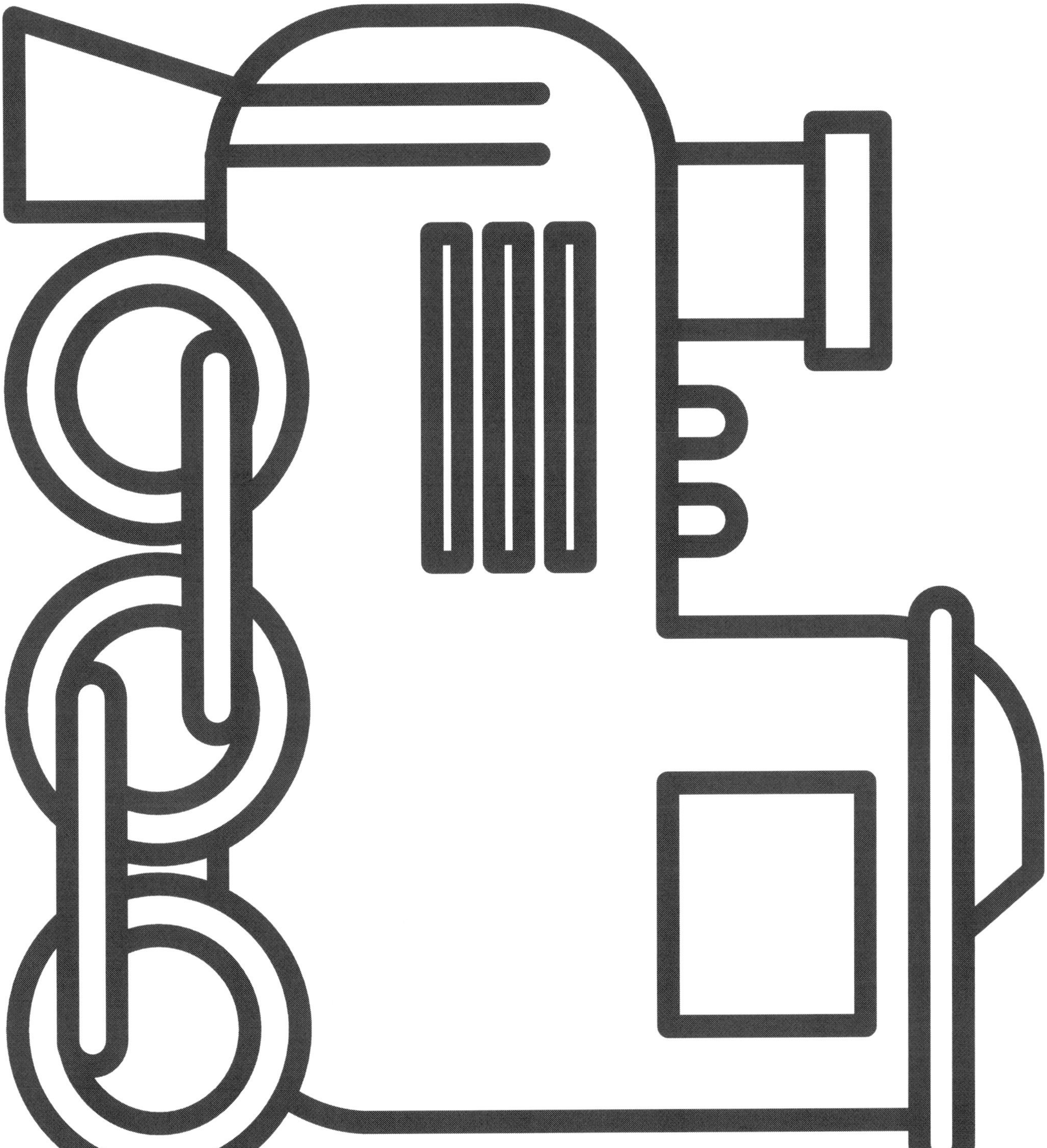

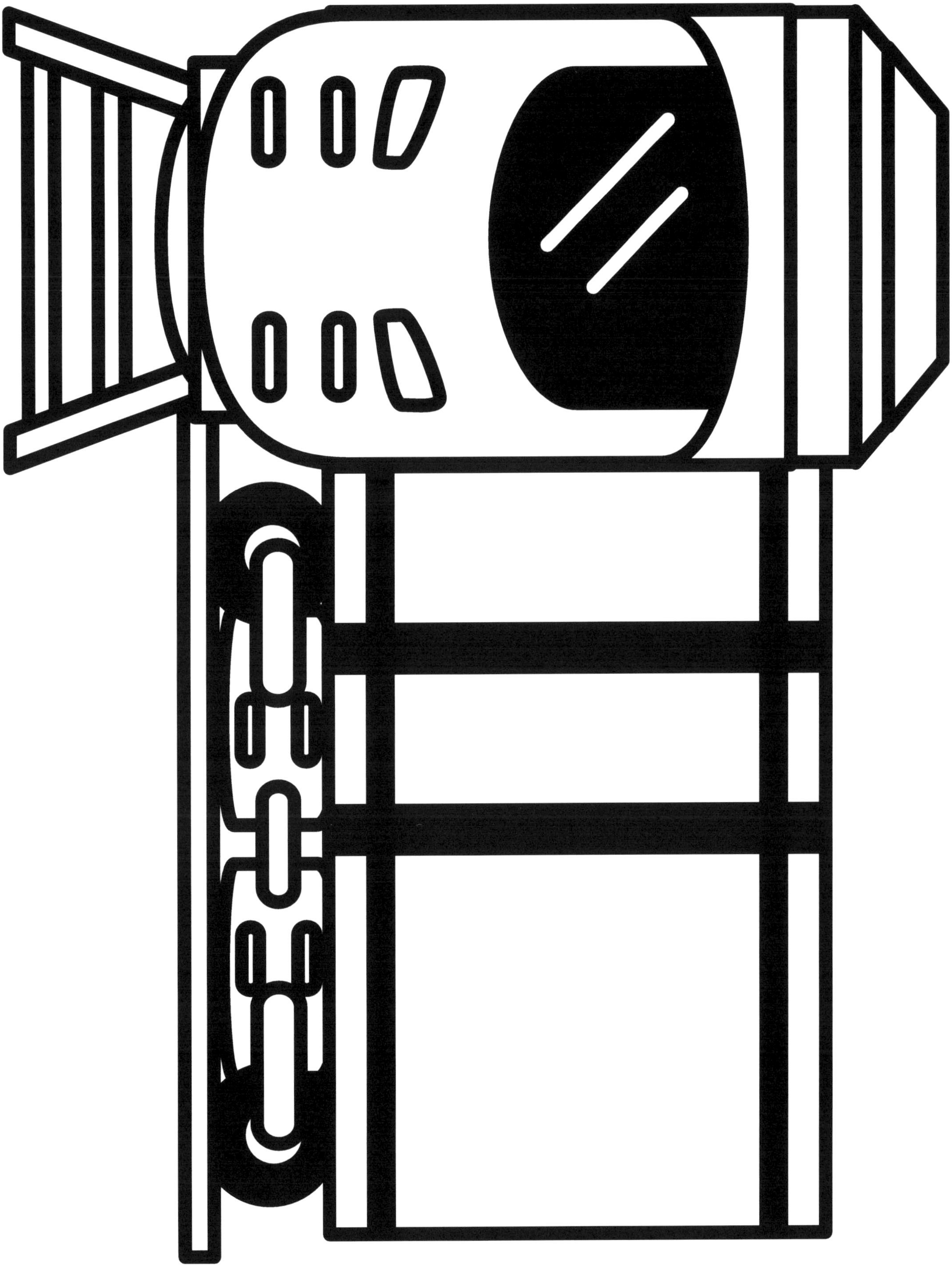

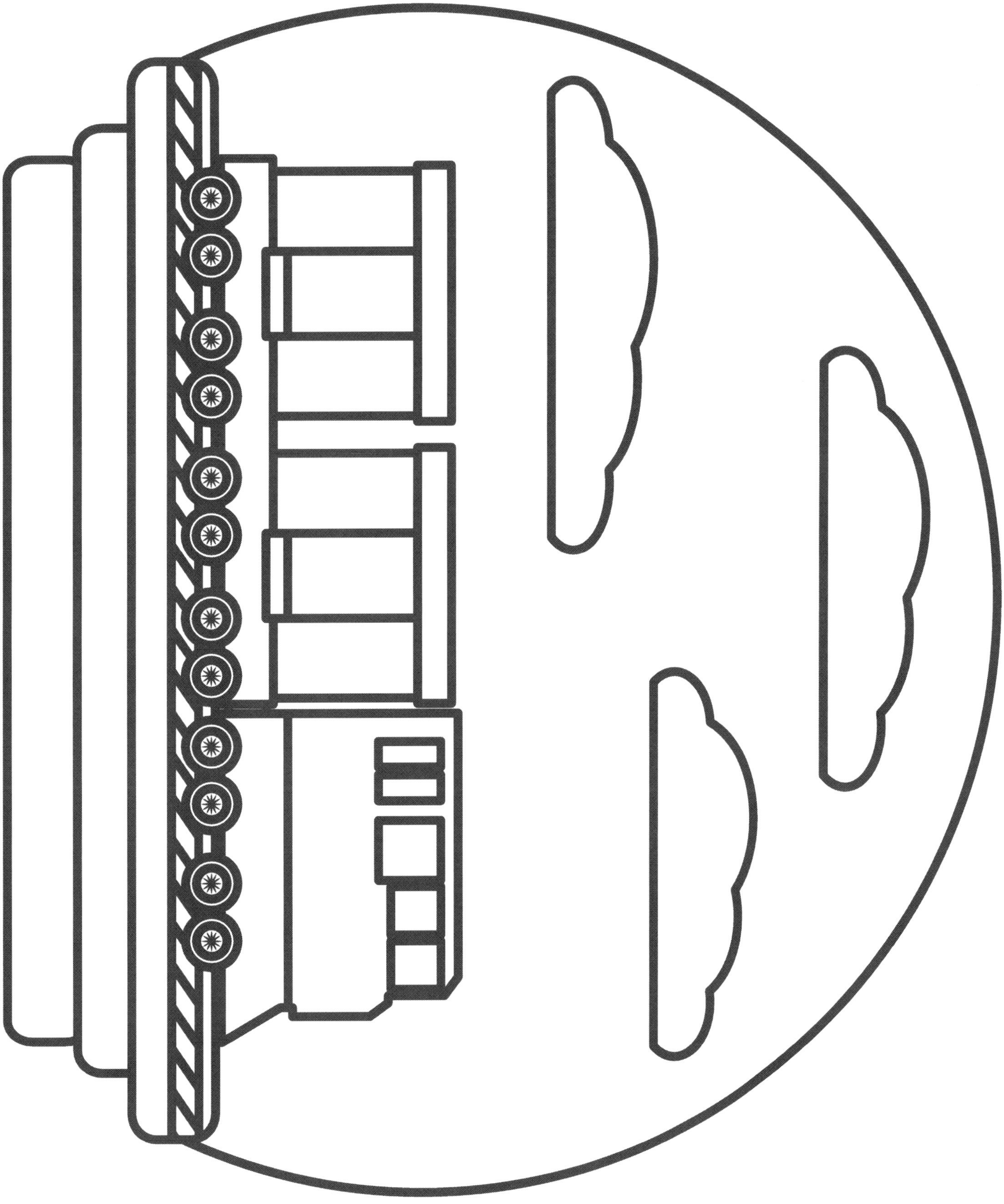

SPARKS IDEA

CREATIVE GENERATION

Manufactured by Amazon.ca
Bolton, ON

24601411R00057